PAKISTAN

R.L. Van

Big Buddy Books
An Imprint of Abdo Publishing
abdobooks.com

abdobooks.com

Published by Abdo Publishing, a division of ABDO, PO Box 398166, Minneapolis, Minnesota 55439. Copyright © 2023 by Abdo Consulting Group, Inc. International copyrights reserved in all countries. No part of this book may be reproduced in any form without written permission from the publisher. Big Buddy Books™ is a trademark and logo of Abdo Publishing.

Printed in the United States of America, North Mankato, Minnesota
102022
012023

Design: Emily O'Malley, Mighty Media, Inc.
Production: Mighty Media, Inc.
Editor: Jessica Rusick
Cover Photograph: Apik/Shutterstock Images
Interior Photographs: AbdulHannan49/Shutterstock Images, p. 27 (bottom); AlexelA/Shutterstock Images, p. 9; Burhan Ay Photography/Shutterstock Images, p. 27 (top right); Chaton Chokpatara/Shutterstock Images, p. 15; Chintung Lee/Shutterstock Images, p. 30 (currency); Derek Brumby/Shutterstock Images, p. 13; Homo Cosmicos/Shutterstock Images, p. 6 (bottom); Hussain Warraich/Shutterstock Images, p. 28 (bottom); ibrar. kunri/Shutterstock Images, p. 6 (middle); Iftekkhar/Shutterstock Images, p. 27 (top left); imagestockdesign/Shutterstock Images, p. 7 (map); Jimmy Tran/Shutterstock Images, p. 19; K_Boonnitrod/Shutterstock Images, p. 26 (right); Kathy Hutchins/Shutterstock Images, p. 21; lev radin/Shutterstock Images, p. 29 (bottom); lukulo/iStockphoto, pp. 5 (compass), 7 (compass); mark reinstein/Shutterstock Images, p. 29 (top); Max Desfor/AP Images, p. 11; nortongo/Shutterstock Images, p. 30 (flag); Pyty/Shutterstock Images, p. 5 (map); Simon Davis/Wikimedia Commons, p. 23; SMDSS/Shutterstock Images, p. 26 (left); thsulemani/Shutterstock Images, p. 17; TripDeeDee Photo/Shutterstock Images, p. 25; Umer Arif/Shutterstock Images, pp. 6 (top), 28 (top)
Design Elements: Mighty Media, Inc.
Country population and area figures taken from the CIA World Factbook

Library of Congress Control Number: 2022940515

Publisher's Cataloging-in-Publication Data
Names: Van, R.L., author.
Title: Pakistan / by R.L. Van
Description: Minneapolis, Minnesota : Abdo Publishing, 2023 | Series: Countries | Includes online resources and index.
Identifiers: ISBN 9781532199714 (lib. bdg.) | ISBN 9781098274917 (ebook)
Subjects: LCSH: Pakistan--Juvenile literature. | Middle East--Juvenile literature. | Asia--Juvenile literature. | Pakistan--History--Juvenile literature. | Geography--Juvenile literature.
Classification: DDC 954.91--dc23

CONTENTS

Passport to Pakistan 4
Important Cities 6
Pakistan in History 8
An Important Symbol 12
Across the Land 14
Earning a Living 16
Life in Pakistan 18
Famous Faces 20
A Great Country 24
Tour Book 26
Timeline 28
Pakistan Up Close 30
Glossary 31
Online Resources 31
Index 32

PASSPORT TO PAKISTAN

Pakistan is a country in South Asia. It borders four countries. About 243 million people live there.

DID YOU KNOW?

Urdu and English are Pakistan's official languages. But many other languages are spoken there.

WHERE IS PAKISTAN?

2

IMPORTANT CITIES

Islamabad is Pakistan's **capital**. It was built in the 1960s. It has parks, forests, and important landmarks.

Karachi is Pakistan's largest city. It is a port and a center of business, transportation, and finance.

Lahore is Pakistan's second-largest city. It is known for its history and culture.

3

PAKISTAN IN HISTORY

People have lived in present-day Pakistan for about 10,000 years. Around 2600 BCE, the Indus civilization developed in the Indus River valley. **Islam** spread in the region starting in the 700s. In the 1800s, the British took control.

More than 5 million people may have lived in the Indus civilization at its height.

In 1947, Britain left the region and split the land. It became Pakistan and India. Pakistan was a homeland for **Muslims**. At first, there was East Pakistan and West Pakistan. In 1971, East Pakistan became Bangladesh. West Pakistan became Pakistan.

Mohammed Ali Jinnah (*left*) fought for Pakistan's independence from Britain. He is sometimes called the father of Pakistan.

AN IMPORTANT SYMBOL

Pakistan's flag is white and green. It has a white moon and star. The moon and star stand for **Islam**.

Pakistan is a **federal parliamentary republic**. The Senate and the National Assembly make laws. The prime minister is head of government. The president is head of state.

Pakistan adopted its flag in 1947.

ACROSS THE LAND

Pakistan has deserts, river valleys, and farmland. The Himalaya and Karakoram mountain ranges are in northern Pakistan.

Bears, leopards, wild goats, and crocodiles live in Pakistan. Acacia shrubs, scrub forests, and fruit trees grow there.

K2 is in Pakistan's Karakoram range. It is the second-highest mountain in the world at 28,251 feet (8,611 m).

6

EARNING A LIVING

Factory workers in Pakistan make clothing, leather, and food products. Many people have service jobs, such as working for the government.

Pakistan's waters provide electricity and fish. Farmers grow wheat, rice, cotton, and fruit. They raise cattle, goats, sheep, and chickens.

Farmers in Pakistan grow mangoes (*pictured*), plums, and guava.

LIFE IN PAKISTAN

Many Pakistanis live in **rural** areas. Popular foods in Pakistan include curry dishes, vegetables, yogurts, and wheat breads. Lemonade, chai tea, and **lassi** are favorite drinks. Cricket, field hockey, and squash are popular sports. Most people in Pakistan are **Muslim**.

Many people in Pakistan buy food at open-air markets.

FAMOUS FACES

Kumail Nanjiani grew up in Karachi. He is a comedian, actor, and writer. In 2017, he co-wrote and starred in *The Big Sick*. The movie was very successful. He has since acted in the movie *Eternals* and the TV show *Obi-Wan Kenobi*.

SAY IT

Kumail Nanjiani
KOO-mile nahn-JA-nee

Kumail Nanjiani attended college in the United States.

Malala Yousafzai was born in Mingora, Pakistan. When she was young, the **Taliban** banned girls in her town from getting an education. Malala was shot for speaking out against this. Thankfully, she survived. At age 17, she received a Nobel Peace Prize. She continues working to help girls go to school.

SAY IT

Malala Yousafzai
muh-LA-la YOO-suhf-zye

Malala Yousafzai was the youngest person in history to receive a Nobel Peace Prize.

A GREAT COUNTRY

Pakistan has beautiful land and a rich history and culture. The people and places of Pakistan help make the world a more interesting place.

> **DID YOU KNOW?**
> Pakistan's national animal is a wild goat called a markhor.

Hunza Valley is often called one of the most beautiful places in Pakistan.

TOUR BOOK

If you ever visit Pakistan, here are some places to go and things to do!

EAT

Taste sweet Pakistani treats like *sheer khurma*, a rice pudding made with dates and milk.

EXPLORE

Go to Faisal **Mosque** in Islamabad. It is Pakistan's national mosque and the largest mosque in South Asia.

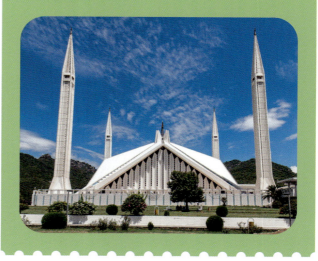

DISCOVER

Visit the ancient city of Harappa along the Indus River.

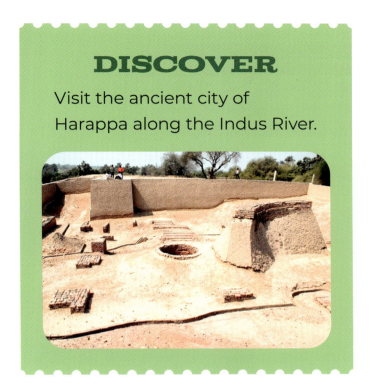

SEE

Wander the historic Shalimar Gardens near Lahore. They were built during the 1600s.

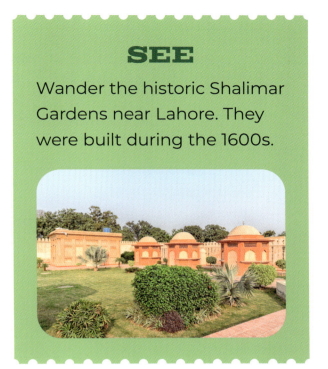

LEARN

Explore the Pakistan Air Force Museum in Karachi. You'll see real airplanes used by the Pakistan Air Force.

TIMELINE

ABOUT 711
Arab **Muslims** brought **Islam** to the area that is now Pakistan.

1856
K2 was measured. It would be nearly 100 years before a person reached the mountain's peak.

1959
Pakistan's government said Islamabad would be built as the **capital**.

1947
Pakistan and India became two nations.

1988

Benazir Bhutto began her term as prime minister of Pakistan. She was the first female leader of a **Muslim** country.

2005

An **earthquake** hit near Islamabad. Roughly 79,000 people died.

2022

Parliament voted Prime Minister Imran Khan out of office. He was the first prime minister of Pakistan to be removed from office by vote.

PAKISTAN UP CLOSE

Official Name
Jamhuryat Islami Pakistan (Islamic Republic of Pakistan)

Flag

Population
242,923,845 (2022 est.)
5th-most-populated country

Total Area
307,374 square miles (796,095 sq km)
36th-largest country

Official Languages
Urdu, English

Capital
Islamabad

Currency
Pakistani rupee

Form of Government
Federal parliamentary republic

National Anthem
"Qaumi Tarana" ("National Anthem")

GLOSSARY

capital—a city where government leaders meet.

earthquake (UHRTH-kwayk)—a shaking of a part of the earth.

federal parliamentary republic—a form of government in which the people choose the leaders. A parliament makes laws. The central government and the individual states share power.

Islam—a religion based on a belief in Allah as God and Muhammad as his prophet.

lassi—a flavored yogurt-based drink popular in India, Pakistan, and other nearby countries.

mosque—a Muslim place of worship.

Muslim—a person who practices Islam.

rural—of or relating to open land away from towns and cities.

Taliban—a violent political and religious group that promotes extreme Islamic beliefs and attacks people to try to force them to accept its beliefs.

ONLINE RESOURCES

To learn more about Pakistan, please visit **abdobooklinks.com** or scan this QR code. These links are routinely monitored and updated to provide the most current information available.

INDEX

animals, 14, 16, 24

Bangladesh, 10
Bhutto, Benazir, 29
businesses, 6, 16

Faisal Mosque, 26
flag, 12, 13, 30
food, 16, 17, 18, 19, 26

government, 12, 16, 29, 30

Harappa, 27
Himalaya mountains, 14
Hunza Valley, 25

India, 5, 10, 28
Indus River, 8, 9, 27
Islam, 8, 10, 12, 18, 28, 29
Islamabad, 6, 7, 26, 28, 29, 30

Jinnah, Mohammed Ali, 11

Karachi, 6, 7, 20, 27
Karakoram mountains, 14, 15
Khan, Imran, 29
K2, 15, 28

Lahore, 6, 7, 27
language, 4, 30

Nanjiani, Kumail, 20, 21
natural resources, 16, 17

Pakistan Air Force Museum, 27
plants, 6, 14, 16, 17, 27
population, 4, 7, 30

Shalimar Gardens, 27
size, 30
South Asia, 4, 26
sports, 18

United Kingdom, 8, 10, 11
United States, 21

Yousafzai, Malala, 22, 23